HUXLEY and ORWELL: BRAVE NEW WORLD AND NINETEEN EIGHTY-FOUR

by

JENNI CALDER

EDWARD ARNOLD

First published 1976 by
Edward Arnold (Publishers Ltd)
41 Bedford Square, London WC1B 3DQ

Reprinted 1982, 1983

ISBN 0 7131 5920 0

*Printed and bound in Great Britain at
The Camelot Press Ltd, Southampton*

COUNTY COUNCIL

Already published in the series:

Already published in the series (*continued*):

General Preface

The object of this series is to provide studies of individual novels, plays and groups of poems and essays which are known to be widely read by students. The emphasis is on clarification and evaluation; biographical and historical facts, while they may be discussed when they throw light on particular elements in a writer's work, are generally subordinated to critical discussion. What kind of work is this? What exactly goes on here? How good is this work, and why? These are the questions that each writer will try to answer.

It should be emphasized that these studies are written on the assumption that the reader has already read carefully the work discussed. The objective is not to enable students to deliver opinions about works they have not read, nor is it to provide ready-made ideas to be applied to works that have been read. In one sense all critical interpretation can be regarded as foisting opinions on readers, but to accept this is to deny the advantages of any sort of critical discussion directed at students or indeed at anybody else. The aim of these studies is to provide what Coleridge called in another context 'aids to reflection' about the works discussed. The interpretations are offered as suggestive rather than as definitive, in the hope of stimulating the reader into developing further his own insights. This is after all the function of all critical discourse among sensible people.

Because of the interest which this kind of study has aroused, it has been decided to extend it first from merely English literature to include also some selected works of American literature and now further to include selected works in English by Commonwealth writers. The criterion will remain that the book studied is important in itself and is widely read by students.

DAVID DAICHES

Contents

Acknowledgements

The Publisher's thanks are due to the following for permission to reproduce copyright material:

Mrs Laura Huxley and Chatto and Windus Ltd for extracts from Aldous Huxley's *Brave New World*, *Brave New World Revisited* and Aldous Huxley's Foreword to the 1946 edition of *Brave New World*; Mrs Sonia Brownell and Secker and Warburg Ltd for extracts from George Orwell's *Nineteen Eight-Four*.

1. Origins and Objects

The idea of utopia has always been a response to the current and the contemporary. Utopia is a way of dealing in the imagination with the problems of the present, although it may be formulated as solutions to the fundamental, perennial problems of men, women and society. Utopia, of course, suggests an ideal. Most of us would shrink from Huxley's vision of the future, all of us from Orwell's, but both of them provide solutions, they both in a sense solve major problems of their own times, although both at the expense of vital features of the quality of human life. They are rational solutions that demonstrate the inadequacy, in fact the horror, of rationality alone.

Brave New World and *Nineteen Eighty-Four* are usually placed in the category of anti-utopian fiction, nightmares not dreams, warnings not portraits of an ideal. Yet both authors were aware that there existed as they were writing processes of thought and action that could lead to what they described, and people who were more than ready to make human sacrifices in order to achieve progress or power. Progress and idealism have always attracted the human race. To be unable to believe that things can and will get better is at best negative, at worst destructive. But to believe that the realization of an ideal is worth any sacrifice, or that progress by its very nature *must* be good for humanity, is extremely dangerous. Orwell and Huxley were both very worried about the tendency towards these beliefs.

The tradition of warning and prophecy is as old as literature itself. In the twentieth century there were writers before Huxley who responded excitedly or fearfully to the possibilities of science and technology. The Victorians had been aware of the havoc caused in the name of progress and some voiced their disapproval, notably Ruskin and William Morris. But H. G. Wells, an early and prolific twentieth-century prophet, had faith in progress, inheriting the more optimistic Victorian belief in technological good while vigorously casting off Victorian restraints and hypocrisy in the area of human behaviour. Although he could foresee societies in the future where things went badly wrong, he was convinced that a combination of science and rightly directed human will could cope. Huxley wasn't so sure. Although he regained to some extent his faith in science as a genuinely progressive force in later life, in the 1930s he was uncomfortably aware that scientists could be irresponsible and dangerous. It was hard not to see the atom bomb as a result, the most dramatic amongst many, of these things.

Another striking prophet of the future was the Russian writer Eugene Zamyatin, whose novel *We* was available in the 1920s though not published in Britain until much later. *We* is a futuristic nightmare, a sterile society, a world clean and organized to the ultimate, enclosed by glass. There are some similarities with both Huxley's and Orwell's versions of the future, and Orwell had certainly read it and praised it. Zamyatin demonstrated the control of man by science; Wells believed that science *could* be controlled by man. I am not concerned with which view now seems more apt or logical, but with the fact that in the post-Victorian years, with the First World War demonstrating some of the implications of technology, there was an immense imaginative interest in the future, in Huxley's case an interest shaped by worry and scepticism and the most acute awareness of disillusion and lack of purpose amongst many of the people whose lives he observed.

If Huxley was sceptical in 1930 when he wrote *Brave New World*, Orwell had almost given up hope in 1948 when he wrote *Nineteen Eighty-Four*. Orwell saw power politics, not science, as the major threat to mankind, and he had had over the previous twelve years or so plenty of opportunity to savour the possibilities of power. In *Nineteen Eighty-Four* he was coping with both a personal and a public depression. His hopes of social revolution now seemed to him illusory. There was a brief period during the war when he had thought there was a genuine movement towards equality, and this had sustained him, but what he saw in the post-war period was defeat in the ashes of victory. The Labour Government elected in 1945 did not seem to be effecting the radical changes Orwell hoped for. His wife was dead. He himself was suffering from the tuberculosis that would soon kill him. He had had the grim experience in 1945 of following the allied armies in their progress through Holland, through France and into Germany and had caught terrible, intimate glimpses of the effects of modern war. His attempt to escape to the

Hebrides and live a solitary and productive life there proved unworkable. The feeling that dominates his book is that it is too late for individuals to halt a process of inevitability that they themselves, in their blindness and selfishness, helped to put in motion. It was not an interest in the possibilities of the future that prompted him to write, but a desperate urge to make a last stand for humanity.

That *Brave New World* and *Nineteen Eighty-Four* are very different in tone and atmosphere no one will contest. A major reason for their difference is, simply, when they were written. What draws them together is the concern the authors share for man and society, and similar reactions to certain specific features of society. Huxley's *Ape and Essence* (1953) is closer both in time of writing and in tone to *Nineteen Eighty-Four* than is *Brave New World*, which is hardly surprising. In the later book he pictures a society that is controlled not by science and manipulation but by crude force. When Huxley wrote to Orwell after reading *Nineteen Eighty-Four* he suggested, in spite of *Ape and Essence* (which most critics agree is not a particularly impressive book), that a more authentic picture of the future would not contain the violence of Orwell's book. It would not be necessary, for men had the means to control the mass of humanity through influencing their minds. That kind of power made the punishment of their bodies unnecessary. In fact, it is not the violence in *Nineteen Eighty-Four* that is the book's most alarming feature, although it is so hard to forget, but the control of the mind through the control of history. In Orwell's Oceania men are manipulated through the manipulation of facts and of the past—although an atmosphere of constant warfare and continual threat is a necessary environment for this manipulation.

That Orwell was using directly the knowledge of methods in Nazi Germany—full knowledge of which only emerged after the war—is obvious. But he was also aware that propaganda in wartime Britain was not essentially different in method from Nazi propaganda. In Oceania there is a state of perpetual crisis which is used as a weapon to get people to do what is wanted, to submit to power. They are persuaded that their own individual interests are identical with the national interest. Exactly the same thing was happening in wartime Britain. Individuals were encouraged to believe that their particular effort, their particular sacrifice, would help to win the war. In a crisis situation things can be asked of people which normally they would find intolerable. Britain won the war, but Orwell felt that the dangers of such a process must not be ignored. In *Nineteen Eighty-Four* he shows ordinary people unquestioningly submitting to an appalling life: Orwell is saying that it could happen in Britain, and that the results would be disastrous.

Descriptions of *Nineteen Eighty-Four* usually concentrate on Orwell's vision of totalitarian power: it is important to point out that he saw in wartime Britain, with emergency powers and a coalition government with no opposition, the seeds of such power. The mechanism of democracy *was* interfered with. The formidable consequences of such interference had occurred in Germany, in Russia, in Spain, in Portugal, but the possibility was everywhere. To Orwell it seemed a very real possibility, and all his writing in those last years of his life has an urgency which may seem to us now, through a perspective of nearly thirty years, to be misplaced. The Cold War has thawed, atomic weapons are, to a certain extent, under international control, we are probably more alert to the flaws in the democratic machinery, affluence has made the drab decay of Oceania seem an unlikely eventuality for eight years from now. But Orwell's urgency was authentic and deeply felt, and the quality of his unelaborate prose convinces us of that. *Brave New World*, more relaxed and satiric, lacks this urgency: it described a very distant future. Many of those alive in 1948 could expect to live to see 1984.

Huxley himself points out one of the significant differences between the two books in his *Brave New World Revisited* (1958). He says,

> George Orwell's *Nineteen Eighty-Four* was a magnified projection into the future of a present that contained Stalinism and an immediate past that had witnessed the flowering of Nazism. *Brave New World* was written before the rise of Hitler to supreme power in Germany and when the Russian tyrant had not yet got into his stride. In 1931 systematic terrorism was not the obsessive contemporary fact which it had become in 1948, and the future dictatorship of my imaginary world was a good deal less brutal than the future dictatorship so brilliantly portrayed by Orwell.

While Huxley acknowledges that Orwell's was an authentic projection he felt, as he had when the book was first published, that the odds were more in favour of his version.

> In the light of what we have recently learned about animal behaviour in general, and human behaviour in particular, it has become clear that

control through the punishment of undesirable behaviour is less effective, in the long run, than control through the reinforcement of desirable behaviour by rewards, and that government through terror works on the whole less well than government through the non-violent manipulation of the environment and of the thoughts and feelings of individual men, women and children.

Huxley felt increasingly that the problems of the world's immediate future would be those of overpopulation and starvation, of the environment and pollution. He was concerned with these issues long before they hit the headlines of public concern. But in the 1920s his worries were about the quality and the purpose of life. We can use his early novels as a guide to an understanding of the post-World War One generation of the privileged classes, their frustrations, their cynicism, their disillusion, their experimentation with different aims in life. Synthetic substitutes for loss of faith recur in his novels. They are peopled with characters who are experiencing post-war (and post-Victorian) disenchantment, to whom it seems only too clear they can no longer believe in the old ways of doing things, in the old social and moral structures, the old artistic conventions, but who are uncertain, in some cases tormented, about what to put in their place. Most of Huxley's characters are unhappy, even those who experiment with the synthetic with some gaiety. In *Brave New World* most of his characters are happy. They have been brainwashed into happiness, and whenever brainwashing cannot wholly work drugs can assist. The difficulties that face the characters in Huxley's contemporary novels have been eliminated, but what is the result? Along with indecision, suffering, human cruelty on a personal level, have been cast out creativity, independence, a sense of self. Individuality, the crux and centre of the human condition, has gone. Orwell's Oceania destroys it too.

In some respects the methods are not so dissimilar. While Huxley's sleeping babies absorb the whispers from tape recorders that determine their attitudes to themselves and others, the Oceanians are bombarded from microphones and telescreens. It is cruder, but essentially the same method. Both writers are reacting against the mindless persuasions of the advertising slogan, and Orwell specifically against the political catchword. Huxley identified advertising as one of the formative influences on modern life. Modern advertising had taken hold in the latter part of the nineteenth century, but it was in its first extravagant flowering in the 1920s. There is a memorable passage in *Eyeless in Gaza* (1936) where the hero as a small boy is travelling in a train past advertisement hoardings. His mood, his feelings, his whole life, seem to be symbolized by the vast and grotesque images he passes. Advertising was not only grotesque and vulgar, a cheapening of responses, it was dangerous, disturbingly powerful, a form of brainwashing. Orwell combines the grotesque and the dangerous in his giant posters of Big Brother that are such an inescapable feature of Airstrip One's drab townscape. In *Brave New World* there is no need for posters, for the work has been done in infancy by the whispering tapes.

Advertising was a direct expression of the capitalist, consumer society ethic and linked with the tyranny of the machine. Reaction against the ugly effects of industrialism was already well established. It was at the core of many of Ruskin and Morris's lectures and essays, and of the latter's *News From Nowhere* (1891). They were both writers who felt with all their being the devastations of industrial society. Right through Huxley's writings Henry Ford is a symbol both of the machine age and of conspicuous consumption, and in *Brave New World* God has become 'Our Ford', money and the machine inexorably linked. Money is one of the problems that the new world has solved, for class is determined in the test tube and possessions are determined by class. There is no competition, no keeping up with the Joneses, no novelties to be grabbed for. The problem has been solved by rationalizing the status quo, confirming inequality in a cleanly scientific way. And it is in the area of science that the radical difference lies between Orwell's and Huxley's books. For Huxley was profoundly worried about the morality of science, about the fact that knowledge could mean power for evil as well as power for good, that science could destroy as well as discover, and about the fact that the more a small body of highly trained men found out about the way human beings function, the more easily could human beings be controlled. Perhaps his greatest fear was that the dangers could occur inadvertently, from the best intentions.

Orwell is worried about the power of totalitarian control, its methods and its effects, but not specifically about the responsibilities of science. The technology of Oceania is no more sophisticated than that which existed in 1948. In terms of science fiction it is crude. There has been no orientation towards making life easier, in fact many of the basic technological aids, lifts for instance, don't work. In Oceania all technological skill goes into the manufacture of armaments in order to perpetuate the state of war that is essential for Big Brother to maintain power. Orwell sees the dangerous potential of science only in terms of overt power, not in terms of the kind of subtle influences in life that Huxley saw as the germs of the control of humanity in the future. Again, the explanation for the difference lies partly in the difference between 1930 and 1948. For Orwell in 1948 the overwhelming fact of existence was the terrible success of totalitarian power, which Hitler's defeat could not wipe out. For Huxley eighteen years earlier it was the lack of spiritual and moral values in a society shaken by its inability to cope with harsh realities and increasingly dominated by technology. The concerns of the two writers are similar, for the quality of life, for human decency, for creativity; it was their identification of the causes of the destruction of what they valued that was inevitably different.

Both Orwell and Huxley regarded the word 'progress' with the greatest suspicion. For Huxley's generation, progress was a word that belonged with the Victorians, and indicated a belief in the inevitable improvement of humanity. Those who had lived through the First War were profoundly sceptical about improvement. What did progress mean to ordinary men and women? How could exciting advances in the laboratory be measured against, for instance, the decline in living standards that post-war unemployment brought? How could the achievement of the dedicated scientist be measured against, for instance, his failure as husband and father, a favourite theme of Huxley's? There were very few who had a thought to spare for the social implications of technological advance, in spite of the fact that the nineteenth century had had a continual problem of the consequences of developing technology. For Orwell, progress could be symbolized negatively by the atom bomb; progress in technological terms meant destruction. Orwell's instincts led him to something like Morris's anti-machine utopia. He found modern technology profoundly distasteful, and revealed very little curiosity about scientific achievement—which always interested Huxley. But although he clearly knew less about what science was doing and could do than Huxley, Orwell shared the feelings of Huxley and many of that generation—he was only ten years younger than Huxley. He was young enough to view the Victorian and Edwardian periods with a nostalgia that Huxley could not share, but old enough to be profoundly affected by the First War's shattering of traditional values. The comfortable faith of the Victorians in the interweaving of progress and Christianity backed by absolute moral values for the continuing improvement of all of mankind worth improving could not be recaptured.

The destruction of belief operated differently on the two men. Huxley turned to a spiritual philosophy which he formulated in later books, and enhanced by his experimentation with drugs. Orwell believed socialism to be the answer, not the socialism propagandized by the theorists, but a socialism based on simple equality, community, and a radical relationship with work and the land. When he was in Spain during the Civil War he had a brief glimpse of what it might be like. It was one of the most important experiences of his life, and should be emphasized as an antidote to the pessimism of *Nineteen Eighty-Four*. Huxley also believed in community. He believed in people coming together, sharing their skills, diversifying their activities, co-operating in their responsibilities, and many of his ideas on these lines can be found in his last novel, *Island* (1962). To find Orwell's more optimistic and positive beliefs in the potential of mankind we must read his journalism and his essays. Too often, *Nineteen Eighty-Four* is read as his final testament. It should be remembered that he deliberately described the bleakest eventuality he could imagine because he so desperately did not want it to happen.

Nineteen Eighty-Four is a political book, and grew out of the political ideas and actions with which Orwell was familiar. *Brave New World* is presented as the logical development of a consumer and technology-orientated society, the means are scientific and the ends are self-perpetuation. It is not obviously political because Huxley foresees the withering away of politics. Once stability is achieved there is no need for politics. In 1946 he wrote a foreword to a new edition where he admitted that he had underestimated developments in atomic research and that the existence of the atomic bomb inevitably changed the shape of the future. The atom bomb (and he wrote this when Orwell was already planning his book) made Orwell's prognostication of a small number of totalitarian states in perpetual warfare a greater possibility. He also felt that developments since he wrote *Brave New World* brought the possibility of a technological utopia a great deal nearer than he had at first foreseen.

Then, I projected it six hundred years into the future. Today, it seems quite possible that the horror may be upon us within a single century.

That is, if we refrain from blowing ourselves to smithereens in the interval. Indeed, unless we choose to decentralize and to use applied science, not as the end to which human beings are to be made the means, but as the means to producing a race of free individuals, we have only two alternatives to choose from: either a number of national, militarized totalitarianisms, having as their root the terror of the atomic bomb and as their consequence the destruction of civilization (or, if the warfare is limited, the perpetuation of militarism); or else one supranational totalitarianism, called into existence by the social chaos resulting from rapid technological progress in general and the atom revolution in particular, and developing, under the need for efficiency and stability, into the welfare-tyranny of Utopia.

This is very close to what in fact Orwell wrote about *Nineteen Eighty-Four*. Fifteen years after *Brave New World* Huxley shares Orwell's feelings that the possibilities for the human race have narrowed. Satire was not the appropriate form for conveying the urgency that Orwell felt, although he had demonstrated his satiric skills a few years before in *Animal Farm* (1945) written during the War when Orwell still felt there was a chance for something like his kind of socialism. In 1931 there was human misery and political betrayal, there was weakness and muddle and hypocrisy, but there was no gargantuan threat. Satire was an appropriate form of exposure and attack. There were six hundred years in which to make sure there would be no brave new world. In 1948 time was running out, for Orwell himself and, he felt, for the human race.

Orwell's language bluntly conveys the possibility of disaster. One senses throughout the book a state of mind that had to dispense with frills and graciousness—although Orwell had always aimed for a style as direct and unadulterated as possible. One of the most impressive aspects of the book is the way in which the style is totally appropriate for the message. There is one moment, when the language can't quite do what is required of it, [the famous rats scene,] but the failure there arises from the choice of an inadequate symbol of the ultimate personal terror. Perhaps the greatest achievement of the book is the way in which Orwell has made language state so plainly, without strain or detectable exaggeration, so devastating a nightmare.

Huxley's touch is lighter. We can admire the sheer cleverness of the book, its cool wit, its finely prepared weapons. But the signs that *Brave New World* should never be read as merely a witty extravaganza are unavoidable. The book has an ugly climax for a very specific purpose. In eight years' time *Brave New World* will be more than half a century old and 1984 will have arrived. It is unlikely that 1984 will make *Nineteen Eighty-Four* irrelevant, or that *Brave New World* will become out of date in the foreseeable future.

2. Plots and People

The striking feature of society in both the novels is uniformity and lack of individualism. In both societies individualism is a threat to the State. Non-corporate behaviour cannot be tolerated. People are categorized, and within the categories there is little to distinguish them. They wear uniforms and they are uniform. In *Nineteen Eighty-Four* Party members, men and women, wear blue overalls. The only necessary distinction is their identification as Party members. In *Brave New World* the colour of the clothes indicates the caste of the wearer, Alpha down to Epsilon, and the lower castes wear less attractive colours than the upper. Conformity is the rule, reinforced by routine and a training that detects the slightest hint of anti-social behaviour. Inevitably, character and personality are also determined by category.

Huxley and Orwell were concerned to demonstrate the dangers of the destruction of individualism, and set out to describe what the absence of individualism could actually mean. But they had to find some way of making their characters interesting, and some way of constructing a plot in which actions would be meaningful. This tends to be a problem of utopian fiction—if life is perfect, or wholly standardized, individual thought and action takes on quite a different relationship to society or the state. It is a problem that has not always been handled successfully, but Orwell and Huxley both solve it in the same way, and solve it in the way Zamyatin had done in *We*. They use rebellion as a means both of exposing the society they describe and of generating characters that have an interest beyond the individualistic and with whom the reader can feel some kinds of identification. Admittedly it is minimal, for while Orwell is demonstrating human nature defeated, Huxley is demonstrating human nature sterilized. Orwell succeeds better in focusing the reader's sympathy, for Huxley's characters are not *aware* of what they have lost while Orwell's Winston Smith becomes increasingly so. Winston's function is crucial, not just as a focus of sympathy, or as a major character furthering the plot, but as a link with 1948 and what we can recognize as normal human feeling and human behaviour. Neither Bernard Marx nor John, the Savage, in *Brave New World* can perform that function. The Savage has an experience of pre-civilization, Bernard of improved civilization, but neither of them have experiences or memories which they can helpfully compare with the present.

Some readers have felt that Winston is too abject a character to carry the weight Orwell places on him, too weak as a rebel and too unsympathetic to retain our concern. Orwell, it has been said, in his insistence on the uncompromising nature of the society he is describing, has gone so far that characterization becomes impossible. It is almost true, yet in spite of its near truth the novel is shatteringly effective, and we remember it not for its details—it is particular features of *Brave New World* that linger in the mind, the test-tube babies, the feelies—but for its overall effect. Winston does do what the author requires of him. Without him as an intimate focus the book would lose most of its power.

In both books the uniformity is suggested in the opening pages. In *Brave New World* the conducted tour around the test tubes is unequivocal. In *Nineteen Eighty-Four* the elements are the drab sameness of the environment, the characterless blocks of flats, the seedy atmosphere suggested by the smell of cabbage and blocked sinks, and humanity itself is just another feature that barely manages to survive in this dreary territory. Winston's vulnerability, his fear, his frailty, his weakness, his capacity for deceit, all emerge as inevitable in terms of the way he has to live, and at the same time, as a trickle of his individuality seeps through, promises only failure if he should take any measures to counteract conformity.

His first act is momentous.

The thing that he was about to do was to open a diary. This was not illegal (nothing was illegal, since there were no longer any laws), but if detected it was reasonably certain that it would be punished by death, or at least by twenty-five years in a forced-labour camp. Winston fitted a nib into the penholder and sucked it to get the grease off. The pen was an archaic instrument, seldom used even for signatures, and he had procured one, furtively and with some difficulty, simply because of a feeling that the beautiful creamy paper deserved to be written on with a real nib instead of being scratched with an ink-pencil. Actually he was not used to writing by hand. Apart from very short notes, it was usual to dictate everything into the speak-write, which was of course impossible for his present purpose. He dipped the pen into the ink and then faltered for just a second. A tremor had gone through his bowels. To mark the paper was the decisive act. (Part One, 1)

This passage reveals some crucial points about Winston and the nature of his rebellion. That it should even occur to Winston to keep a diary is significant, for in Oceania the past is not a question of recorded fact which once set down is permanent, but of constant manipulation and obliterations. History is always in the process of being rewritten, so that for Winston to set down a private record is both quixotic and dangerous. To put down on paper words which are not subject to the scrutiny and alteration of the Party is a political act. To write in a notebook that dates from before Ingsoc with an 'archaic' pen, objects from a past which has been obliterated, is a political act. And the act takes some courage—the consequences of discovery are made clear.

But there is more to Winston and his rebellion than this. His rebellion is at this stage instinctive. Although he understands what might be the consequences of his act, he does not understand politics, or history. He is aware of the attraction the proles have for him, of his inclination to spend time alone, of the attraction of the 'beautiful creamy paper' of the notebook he bought in a prole shop, and he knows that his response to these things is dangerous. But he has not related it to anything larger. It is a very small, very personal rebellion, and in fact it is never anything more. What Orwell is telling us is that the smallest and most personal of rebellions can damage the fabric of Ingsoc even if it is confined to the individual. Which is why the Party cannot allow the individual any sense that he is acting independently of their dictates.

The writing in the diary reflects also Winston's almost unconscious desire to discover the past. He can only guess at the date. Time doesn't mean anything as it has nothing to relate to either in the past or in the future. Winston tries to bring to the surface dim memories of his mother, his childhood, what life was like before the revolution. They are not happy memories, they can serve only as images of the past, the nearest he can get to confirmation that the past really existed. This initiation of Winston's rebellion contains in it all the crucial elements. It is an anti-social act, for it is an expression of individuality. It is a historical act, for it seeks to discover the past. And it is a sensual act, in the pleasure that the pen and notebook can provide. The rest of the book extends and substantiates these elements of his rebellion, until the moment of his arrest, when the promise of defeat, which we are never allowed to forget, is fulfilled.

Winston's frailty is emphasized at the outset. He is small, his body 'meagre', a varicose ulcer on his ankle and, although only thirty-nine, he has to take the stairs slowly with frequent rests. The contrast with the enormous face on the poster is immediate. What chance has the meagre Winston against the 'ruggedly handsome features' of the ever-watchful Big Brother? The contrast is extended. O'Brien is a solid, well-built man. Julia is healthy and athletic. Even as Winston's rebellion is developing, his physical inadequacy is always in evidence, and the increased physical well-being which his affair with Julia brings is only an ironic preparation for his final defeat.

The first part of the book establishes Winston's lack of adjustment to the demands of Ingsoc, and at the same time demonstrates the power the Party has over him. It is not just the paraphernalia of telescreens and Thought Police that exercise that power, but something much deeper and more dangerous. It is a psychological power, a power that can, for instance, induce Winston to participate in the Two Minutes Hate with every fibre of his being in spite of his resistance to it.

> In a lucid moment Winston found that he was shouting with the others and kicking his heel violently against the rung of his chair. The horrible thing about the Two Minutes Hate was not that one was obliged to act a part, but, on the contrary, that it was impossible to avoid joining in. Within thirty seconds any pretence was always unnecessary. A hideous ecstasy of fear and vindictiveness, a desire to kill, to torture, to smash faces in with a sledge-hammer, seemed to flow through the whole group of people like an electric current, turning one even against one's will into a grimacing, screaming lunatic. (Part One, 1)

With this kind of power, the power to manipulate the worst in human nature (and that the violence *is* in human nature Orwell recognizes) the Party is surely undefeatable, except by an equally violent force. Orwell himself accepted only reluctantly and after a period of pacifism the necessity to counter Fascism by force and in *Nineteen Eighty-Four* he is exploring some of the implications of this. In Oceania we can see the process of violence breeding violence. When he is prevented from sitting next to Julia in the canteen, Winston imagines himself 'smashing a pick-axe right into the middle' of the face of the man responsible. (Part II, 1) It is not only under the influence of the Two Minutes Hate that images of violence dominate his mind. He has been thoroughly infected by the Party ethic, primed to accept O'Brien's ultimate justification of power, in spite of the fact that he is trying so hard to rediscover his humanity.

Winston's attempt to do this ripples out from the moment when he first sets pen to paper. He wanders alone in the prole districts and in the savouring of the dirt and the squalor finds a quality of human life that is both abhorrent and attractive. The life of the proles, 'the swarming disregarded masses', is indescribably squalid (Orwell does of course describe it) but they have a degree of freedom which is unthinkable for Party members. There are no telescreens. Winston catches a whiff of real coffee (acquired on the black market). In the junk shop are real, tangible objects that date from pre-revolution days. His interest in these things is dangerous. Even walking on his own is an anti-social act, although to have shared his walks with one other person would have been even worse. A meaningful personal relationship which is not dominated by the Party is criminal. So is a taste for solitude, *ownlife* in Newspeak, which could indicate dangerous individualism. Winston commits both these crimes, and with their commitment becomes conscious that they constitute a political act.

It is that consciousness which is all-important, for without it his rebellion would be of little importance—as Julia's is. Julia's crime is that her frank sexuality is unpermissible, but she sees her rebellion merely in personal terms, and she sees the Party's authority only in terms of how it restricts her wants. Winston's awareness is crucial because it articulates and individualizes his rebellion. In a sense it is the thinking that counts more than the doing, as the mere existence of the Thought Police might suggest. Winston is first lured into exposing his thoughts, then he is cured of them. That he has been acting rebelliously the Party has clearly known for a long time. He is arrested when he knows that he is thinking rebelliously and with deliberate purpose. He is taught how to 'think right' in Party terms, and therein lies his defeat, and the terrible pessimism of the book.

Winston's self-awareness, through which he can exercise something like individuality, intensifies from the point when he begins his diary and is seeking a context for revolt. Julia is a catalyst rather than a fellow conspirator. As they gradually make cautious arrangements to come together Winston's capacity for intense feeling and excitement grows, and he discovers himself capable of a new dimension of response.

> His whole mind and body seemed to be afflicted with an unbearable sensitivity, a sort of transparency, which made every movement, every sound, every contact, every word that he had to speak or listen to, an agony. Even in sleep he could not altogether escape from her image. (Part Two, 1)

That Winston is able to feel like this is important, for it is his strength, a demonstration of human susceptibilities. That he can feel, that he can worry about another human being, that he can experience sexual desire, all these are plusses in his function as a link between Oceania and normality, Oceania and the present, both our present and 1948. His defeat may be implicit in the opening of the book, but he is not yet defeated. Yet ironically his capacity for thought and experience reinforces the certainty that the worst that can happen to him will happen to him: the value of his rebellion, the value of his relationship with Julia and his brief enactment of independence, will be wiped out of his mind. He will be left with nothing. It is not just that he fails politically that matters (there is nothing of the true revolutionary or leader in his make-up) but even more that he loses every vestige of his personality that contained genuine humanity. It is precisely this capacity that causes his downfall.

The relationship with Julia is, of course, not at all satisfactory. The circumstances under which it is conducted would hardly allow it to be, but its lack is contained more fundamentally in Julia herself and in Winston's unwillingness to accept her inadequacy. He needs her, but politically she can be of no use to him. Julia has no interest in the political aspect of their actions, although she is acute in her understanding of the ways of the Party and she realises why her sexuality cannot be tolerated. She wants to escape the power of the Party, not attack it. Her communication with Winston is almost entirely sexual, and although that is important, as the love-making scenes in the almost dream land of the countryside and the womb-like interior of the room above the junk shop emphasize, it is not enough. Escape, private satisfaction, is not enough, and Winston's recognition of this, though it gets him nowhere, contains a kind of heroism. At the end of the book he has been forced to deny the value of heroism, but why deny it if it does not contain some vestige of meaning and hope? We must recognize it as meaningful if the book is to have anything of more than negative value to say. We have to see Winston's rebellion as an end in itself, as a significant human gesture, not just as possible means doomed to failure in the pursuit of ends.

Huxley was also very much concerned with ends and means. He argued, in a number of essays as well as in *Island*, that individuals were ends in themselves, not means to ends, nationalistic, militaristic, commercial, or whatever. In *Brave New World* people are means, not ends; their only real value is in their function. We cannot seriously read *Nineteen Eighty-Four* as an existentialist text, but if we are to read it as anything other than a heavily pessimistic reaction to a possible version of political reality we must be aware of the way in which Orwell authenticates the worth of Winston's rebellion. Orwell fills out the relationship between Winston and Julia, the centre of the rebellion, by introducing elements that he himself considered genuine and real. The thrush and its song, the sunlight, the bluebells are suggestive presences during their first meeting in the country, and almost allow us to forget the threat and the possibility of hidden microphones amongst the natural beauties of the countryside. But it is not just aspects of nature that Orwell uses. Julia brings with her *real* chocolate: later, in Mr Charrington's room, they drink real coffee with real sugar, and eat real bread with real jam. Orwell found the whole idea of the synthetic deeply offensive. There is a memorable scene in *Coming Up for Air* (1939) when George Bowling bites into a synthetic sausage and is overcome with disgust. For Orwell the synthetic was a sign of moral deterioration. The fact that Julia's use of make-up is also a part of this 'reality' might seem a contradiction, but it is important because, in Winston's eyes, it enhances her femininity, and therefore her sexuality, and a crucial part of their relationship is natural sexuality. The Party discourages femininity, and the hearty, robust image Julia adopts is for the Party's benefit. '"In this room I'm going to be a woman, not a Party comrade".' Julia says. It helps them, Winston particularly as he is trying to regain a sense of the past, to rediscover what humanity has lost.

A yellow ray from the sinking sun fell across the foot of the bed and lighted up the fireplace, where the water in the pan was boiling fast. Down in the yard the woman had stopped singing, but the faint shouts of children floated in from the street. He wondered vaguely whether in the abolished past it had been a normal experience to lie in bed like this, in the cool of a summer evening, a man and a woman with no clothes on, making love when they chose, talking of what they chose, not feeling any compulsion to get up, simply lying there and listening to peaceful sounds outside. (Part Two, 4)

Winston is trying to reconstruct an understanding of normality, but the freedom here is illusory, the pleasure cannot last—Orwell never lets us forget the vulnerability not just of the relationship but of the quality of their feelings. The vulnerability is there because this cannot be just a personal affair, and because it would never have existed without its extra-personal function. They don't come together simply as a man and woman attracted to each other, but as people who have each recognized the maladjustment in the other.

Inevitably the steps are taken to politicize their rebellion, though not with much interest on Julia's part, but the attack on Winston after his arrest is on his new-found humanity rather than his politics. It is not political theory or belief that matters so much as commitment to a decent way of life. One of the points that Orwell is trying to make is that what destroys Winston is brutality and degradation, and if the essential humanity of a man, his decent instincts and feelings, are destroyed then he is nothing. At the end of the book Winston is alive but he is nothing. He has been forced to deny everything he might ever have valued. Physically he is a wreck, but it is his mental degradation that is the Party's crucial achievement, for O'Brien makes Winston see as truths precisely those things he had recognized as distortions.

The process of breaking Winston down, which some readers have found unconvincing, is the necessary demonstration of the possibilities of power, and without such a demonstration Orwell's warning would be without its urgent effect. He has to show us that the will, the mind and the body can all be destroyed without destroying life itself, and he has to show us, also, that the victim in fact co-operates with his persecutors, that the degradation is, in a sense, voluntary. Orwell had clearly partially based this on what he knew of the operation of the Moscow Trials, through which Stalin conducted his purges. The collaboration between victim and persecutor had been documented in several places, and Koestler had based his memorable *Darkness at Noon*, which impressed Orwell, on this. Winston wants to do what O'Brien demands. He sees O'Brien as an almost fatherly protector, someone with Winston's welfare at heart, and he yearns to be able genuinely to do the right thing. He virtually asks for his final dose of treatment in Room 101, in his reminder to O'Brien that so far he has escaped it, that he has not betrayed Julia.

It might be argued that in terms of the reduction of Winston's personality and the dramatic tension of the narrative the penultimate stage of Winston's treatment is a more effective climax than the questionable episode of the rats. Although rats are Winston's ultimate fear, and this has been already demonstrated, it is hard to believe that they could be worse than the experiences Winston has already had at the hands of the power machine, or that, although the betrayal of Julia is essential to the Party's purpose, it could not have been achieved by the same means as Winston's other submissions. At the same time it should be emphasized that it is the betrayal of Julia, of another human being with whom Winston had established an extra-Ingsoc relationship, that is crucial. Ultimately the message of *Nineteen Eighty-Four* is not political in the narrow sense. It does not uphold or refute a particular body of ideas. It is anti-authoritarian, anti-élite, against the concentration of power, against any tendency that might work against a creative, stimulating atmosphere in which the individual can flourish. He always hoped that equality and sharing and cooperation might be a spontaneous development of human nature, like that which he had briefly experienced in Spain, and that the necessity for power-based politics might be superseded altogether. Orwell's brand of socialism attacked the whole idea of power-based politics. This is the positive movement that lies behind the pessimism of *Nineteen Eighty-Four*. Winston has to betray Julia because he has to deny all that is best in humanity. But at the same time I think it is just possible to argue that Orwell is alerting us, as he does elsewhere in his writing, to the potential of positive human qualities. If the values symbolized by the thrush and the real coffee and the good bread are retained, values that have everything to do with simple, unadulterated experience, then there is still hope.

Winston as a character cannot carry the weight of even a small germ of hope; we have to glean this from moments in the book where Orwell's own beliefs in certain elementary values come through. That he could not exclude them entirely from the book is significant. In some respects *Brave New World* contains fewer indications of optimism than *Nineteen Eighty-Four*. The blandness of *Brave New World* is more suffocating, though less terrifying. Huxley's society is so much more efficient and has tamed human nature to a much greater extent. The conditioned, synthetic society of *Brave New World* allows even less scope for individualism than Ingsoc and Oceania do, and in fact the only character whose fate the reader can care about to any extent is the Savage, whose origins are quite different from those of the citizens of the new world. It is the Savage who, in the end, personifies the rebellion most adequately, for Bernard Marx, who reveals rebellious symptoms, is too much the product of his conditioning. He is the necessary link with the Savage Reservation—it is his intelligent oddness that generates his interest in the savages—but he is not himself a genuine rebel.

A rebel could only be the result of a mistake, for conditioning in test tube and infancy ensures the stability of *Brave New World*'s caste-structured society. Stability is the key word. Where Orwell imagines a situation where the maintaining of power for its own sake is the goal of the élite's existence, Huxley envisages a state of continuous consumption that is the object of life and society. 'Ending is better than mending,' is the slogan. Things must be used up and thrown away and replaced. It contains all the logic of built-in obsolescence and conspicuous consumption, and the function of each individual of each caste is a means to this end. Conditioning enables everyone to accept his or her role, and engineering reinforces their contentment. The instruments of the engineering are sex and *soma*. The uncontented, like Bernard Marx, are oddities, and the strength of framework and conditioning is such that there is no chance of oddity developing into rebellion. There is a mechanism for dealing with oddity: it is not destroyed, merely removed to somewhere where it is harmless and cannot infect others. Only the Savage has something of a chance to make a choice between the new world and the old, and destroys himself because his attempt at compromise, an attempt to create a little island of old in the midst of the new, cannot possibly succeed.

Before we are introduced to the possibility of non-conformity Huxley establishes the structure of stability, and establishes at the same time, as

Orwell does, the unlikelihood of revolt. Conditioning is such that in the case of someone displaying disquieting indications of individuality, the other members of the group will automatically put on the pressure to conform. When we meet Lenina Crowne this is what is happening. She has displayed an unacceptable propensity to stick to one man. ' "It's such horribly bad form to go on and on like this with one man," ' her friend Fanny says when Lenina admits that she has been going out with the same man exclusively for four months. Lenina admits her fault and promises to try to be more promiscuous. Lenina is not a serious non-conformist. She does not have the sensitivities of Bernard and has absolutely no wish to discover anything beyond the life she knows. There is no pain in her situation, and although she acts as a useful catalyst in the plot, her role has less importance than Julia's. Her most useful function is to demonstrate the female sex role in the stability system.

Huxley makes us rapidly aware of the fact that natural feelings and attachments have been wiped out. Words like marriage, monogamy, family and childbirth are unmentionable, signs of the hideous crudities of the past. The family was a breeding ground for squalid, intense relationships, extremes of love and aggression, which can have no place in a stable society. And society is not only stable, it is synthetic. Nothing is natural, everything is surrogate. Everything is man-made. Bernard's inclination to walk in the Lake District or to relish the effects of bad weather on the sea is considered by others to be rather disgusting. There is a suggestion of the primitive about it. The whole fabric of life is synthetic, synthetic materials, synthetic music, synthetic food, these are the substance and the comforts of life. The natural is abhorrent.

This is what stability has cured.

Mother, monogamy, romance. High spurts the fountain; fierce and foamy the wild jet. The urge has but a single outlet. My love, my baby. No wonder those poor pre-moderns were mad and wicked and miserable. Their world didn't allow them to take things easily, didn't allow them to be sane, virtuous, happy. What with mothers and lovers, what with the prohibitions they were not conditioned to obey, what with the temptations and the lonely remorses, what with all the diseases and the endless isolating pain, what with the uncertainties and the poverty—they were forced to feel strongly (and strongly, what

was more, in solitude, in hopelessly individual isolation), how could
they be stable? (Chapter 3)

Not only individuality but isolation are seen as dangerous and dreadful.
In the new world, too, *ownlife* is a disturbing concept. Stability has wiped
out pain, but it has also wiped out all the most valuable human instincts
and actions, as Huxley demonstrates. His society is both logical and
technologically achievable, and his diagnosis of, for instance, the horrors
of introverted family tension, is apt, but his improvements are at the
expense of pretty much the same qualities that Ingsoc has wiped out. It is
hard not to be overwhelmed by the boredom of life in the brave new
world—except that we know its citizens have been conditioned not to
feel bored. There is plenty to do, although little variety, and doing is
encouraged within specific controls. But the uniformity of the activities,
the surroundings, and the people themselves affect the quality of action.
There is no spontaneity and there are no extremes of pleasure. Bernard, in
his struggle to make something positive of his individuality, can find no
scope or outlet for it. The language doesn't exist, the feeling scarcely
exists—shouldn't exist. Privacy is almost impossible. Huxley, in his
awareness of the power of the pressures to conform in society, in any
society, is conveying something as important as Orwell's understanding
of the operation of power politics.

The repetition of life in the brave new world, the repetition of
activities, personalities, slogans, conversations, is one of the most
devastating aspects of stability. There can't be change or variety, and
even progress is something that *has* happened, not something that *will*
happen. Time has no meaning. History has no meaning. The future is as
irrelevant as the past. Without time and the past and an anticipation of the
future, where is the individual? In Oceania this necessary environment
for the individual has also been destroyed. But on the Savage Reservation
and amongst the proles this environment does still exist. Huxley's
characterization of life amongst the savages, with their religion and their
rituals, is more specific than Orwell's of the proles, for the proles are
presented as wholly demoralized, the victims of the oligarchy, while the
savages are left to pursue their own life as long as they don't escape and
infiltrate civilization. John, the Savage, is sustained by strong social
feelings as well as by Shakespeare. Winston is groping for
sustenance—he has no experience of an alternative. When he goes

amongst the proles in search of the old life he finds no consciousness of what the past might mean. He asks leading questions and receives uncomprehending, trivial answers.

We see Bernard, and perhaps Lenina, as potential non-conformists, if not as actual rebels. Bernard is aware that he doesn't fit in, and is told by the Director that it is very important that he should.

> My workers must be above suspicion, particularly those of the highest castes. Alphas are so conditioned that they do not *have* to be infantile in their emotional behaviour. But that is all the more reason for their making a special effort to conform. It is their duty to be infantile, even against their inclination. (Chapter 6)

But it is *conditioning* that makes such an appeal effective, and although the threat of punishment is there also it is on quite a different level than that of *Nineteen Eighty-Four*. And again it is conditioning that allows punishment to be a secondary and far from drastic weapon. Bernard is helpless not because he will be crushed, but because there is no answer to a social structure that maps out the course of human life in the test tube.

In *Nineteen Eighty-Four* an enemy is necessary, for hatred and aggression are the cohesive forces that make Ingsoc work. There has to be a common focus of hatred, although the objects of hatred are essentially no different from the haters. In *Brave New World* there is no need for enemies, because conformity and acceptance are the cohesive factors, and this is one of the reasons why individuality is out of place rather than dangerous. It is hard to feel any great interest in Lenina or Bernard or any other character in *Brave New World*. The Savage is the only man of substance and he is a curious composite of a primitive upbringing and an intimate acquaintance with Shakespeare. For all the debility of Winston, Huxley's characters are much flatter than Orwell's (and tend to be in his other satiric works) and he has to employ more schematic methods of describing the essential features of his new society. Scientific detail plays a much greater part in Huxley's book, and there is always a problem of finding a suitable narrative method to convey it. Characters have to be used as vehicles. And they have to be, even trickier, simultaneously the objects of satire and the instruments of satire. Huxley handles this problem to a certain extent by using two characters, the Director and the Controller, as means of explaining the context of the narrative. Their elevation means that they have a grasp of the mechanism of stability which the other characters cannot have. At the same time, they cannot be allowed to be beyond its control.

At the beginning of the book the Director is showing students around the Central London Hatchery and Conditioning Centre, which allows the whole process of test tube breeding and conditioning to be explained. He can adopt the tone of a teacher to the uninitiated, but a teacher who maintains his reverence for the system he explains. He is explaining the workings of a wonderful system that has created a perfect society, and his attitude is, must be, wholly conformist. Even the Controller, who has greater leeway and can use words such as 'mother' and 'marriage' without flinching, has to be within the system. His greater consciousness of the differences between old and new and his greater understanding of rebellion cannot be allowed to place him outside the control of stability.

The Controller's position, the Director's explanations, and the unorthodoxy of Bernard are all means of indicating how and why conformity is essential to stability, and what stability in fact is. The Savage is another instrument of illustrating the nature of the new society, another angle of observation which actually encompasses something of the past. In all this there is scope for illustration but there is also scope for satire and sheer comedy. There are frequent moments in *Brave New World* where the reader laughs outright, and this of course affects the response to character. Are we really meant to be taking it all seriously? Yet, though *Brave New World* is funny and *Nineteen Eighty-Four* most certainly isn't, they both have similarly violent climaxes which are in both cases consummations of the anti-individualistic character of the societies they describe. Winston's personality is destroyed. The Savage, unable either to adapt or effectively rebel, kills himself. Bernard, who has an instinct to rebel but can't realize it, goes through exactly the same process of demoralization and betrayal that is forced on Winston, although the degree is very different. Bernard also grovels and begs to avoid punishment and loses all self-respect. But drastic methods are not needed to put Bernard in his place: a few grains of *soma* and later despatch out of harm's way are all that is necessary.

Positive identity, extremes of action, intense feeling, and all the misery and confusion that these entail, are the sole property of the Savage. His isolation is terrible. The climactic orgy, the flagellation and the suicide are very convincing, for they are the eruption of the Savage's solitary confusions and unorthodoxies. He cannot survive in the sterile world of stability. Suicide, an ironic indication of choice and self-identity, is the price he has to pay for his humanity. The significance lies in the fact that Huxley has to show the destruction of an outsider, after his attack from outside, rather than the destruction of an insider after an attempt to rebel from within. It is the latter that Orwell describes. In the brave new world there could be no rebels, yet a rebellion was essential to Huxley's purpose of exposure.

3. Human Nature

Huxley and Orwell both present warnings based on how human nature might be destroyed. Towards the end of both books there is some reflection on the fact that heroism has become meaningless. Not only have traditional qualities of courage and daring become irrelevant, but all the best qualities of humanity have lost their place and function. That a combination of technology and organization has the potential of removing human suffering cannot be denied. That it might in the process remove a great deal more, perhaps aspects of humanity that, lost, would make human beings unrecognizable, is a chilling speculation.

In Chapter 16 of *Brave New World* Huxley puts into the mouth of the Controller an explanation of exactly what has happened in the process of constructing utopia. Instability has been removed, chance and fluctuation have been removed, and the implications are formidable. '"You can't make tragedies without social instability,"' the Controller says.

> 'The world's stable now. People are happy; they get what they want, and they never want what they can't get. They're well off; they're safe; they're never ill; they're not afraid of death; they're blissfully ignorant of passion and old age; they're plagued with no mothers or fathers; they've got no wives, or children, or loves to feel strongly about; they're so conditioned that they practically can't help behaving as they ought to behave. And if anything should go wrong. there's *soma*.' (Chapter 16)

Tragedy, worry, suffering have all gone. All the components of life's daily difficulties have been removed. But so, also, have all the major influences that characterize human life. Where would poetry and painting be without love and death? It is not a simplistic equation, suffering equals the production of great art, but a question of the value of experience, and the value of life without experience. Even the happiness that the Controller claims as the great achievement can have no intensity.

To imagine human nature flourishing in this bland and sterile context is impossible.

Unlike the other characters, the Controller is aware of what has been lost. Happiness in the past, he argues, has been no more than 'overcompensations for misery'. And he realizes that 'stability isn't nearly as spectacular as instability. And being contented has none of the glamour of a good fight against misfortune, none of the picturesqueness of a struggle with temptation, or a fatal overthrow by passion or doubt.' Hygienic happiness has replaced picturesque squalor, and picturesque happiness. The implication is that this is the only way of getting rid of the squalor. Shakespeare has to be sacrificed for the good of mankind.

But mankind has to be sacrificed too. In order to maintain stability, intelligence and imagination must be conditioned and controlled. The Deltas and Epsilons are necessary, not only to provide a section of the population that will contentedly perform the necessary menial tasks, but to balance the Alphas. Without Alphas, Epsilons would be meaningless, and vice versa. A society composed entirely of Alphas—'separate and unrelated individuals of good heredity and conditioned so as to be capable (within limits) of making a free choice and assuming responsibilities'—would be disastrous. The Controller has to make this point. The Alphas are the privileged, aware of themselves as privileged but not regarded as such by the others, who retain all that can be allowed of human nature. When they get together in an independent situation the 'Cyprus experiment' is the result.

> The Controllers had the island of Cyprus cleared of all its existing inhabitants and re-colonized with a specially prepared batch of twenty-two thousand Alphas. All agricultural and industrial equipment was handed over to them and they were left to manage their own affairs. The result exactly fulfilled all the theoretical predictions. The land wasn't properly worked; there were strikes in all the factories; the laws were set at naught, orders disobeyed; all the people detailed for a spell of low-grade work were perpetually intriguing for high-grade jobs, and all the people with high-grade jobs were counter-intriguing at all costs to stay where they were. Within six years they were having a first class civil war. (Chapter 16)

In other words, human nature is quarrelsome, competitive, aggressive, selfish, and the brave new world has removed the possibility for people to show themselves at their worst. What Huxley does not discuss is the possibility that some outlet for the aggressive instinct might be as necessary as an outlet for the sexual instinct to maintain stability.

The heights have been removed from human existence, but so have the depths. Huxley presents the dilemma with the utmost clarity, and if his characters lack the substance we look for in fiction, they demonstrate unequivocally the nature of a society without fiction. Mustapha Mond, the Controller, is himself a character worth pausing over, for he is the man of intelligence and understanding who has to be the exception that proves the rule. Neither Bernard nor his friend Helmholtz, superlatively Alpha Plus though he be, would be capable of interpreting the brave new world for the benefit of the Savage in the way the Controller can. Bernard is not aware of the full implications of his introduction of the Savage to civilization, for either party. Mond was given the choice, at an earlier stage in his career, between rebellion—and exile—and responsibility, and chose the latter with a certain regretful lingering over what the former might have contained for him. His function is the same as that of Orwell's O'Brien. They are both the high priests of rationalism on the terms demanded by the society they serve. But they are instruments, and they have to recognize the limitations of their power. Without their acceptance of subservience, to an Idea greater than human, or at least greater than their own concept of themselves, their means of power would vanish. In loving Big Brother, Winston can vicariously share Big Brother's power at the same time as forgoing all the pain of responsibility. He is collaborating precisely in the way the Party requires. In choosing responsibility the Controller is doing the same thing. He is accepting the structure of authority. Orwell and Huxley both show how easy it is for human nature, even in spite of itself, to be enwrapped by the system. The insidious attractions of power are not just for those who want to wield it, but also for those who want to feel its influence. The theme is particularly Orwell's, for he saw it happen.

Huxley saw the power contained by science, and by scientists who could not resist applying the knowledge they had gained, regardless of possible results. But science can destroy not only 'old fashioned' human nature but new stability, so science must be used to control science. '"The Inventions Office is stuffed with plans for labour-saving processes,"' Mond says. But they can't be used, for already the ideal working week and the ideal working conditions have been put into practice, and increased leisure would be disastrous. "'It would be sheer cruelty to inflict them with excessive leisure"' Mond explains. And change itself is a 'menace to stability'. Once stability has been achieved change is anathema, and as change is generally the result of human imagination and striving, these qualities are not only irrelevant, but dangerous. '"Every discovery in pure science is potentially subversive; even science must sometimes be treated as a possible enemy."'

The Controller's explanations are necessary, but while they crystallize the issues contained in the novel they inevitably draw attention to an aspect that Huxley ignores: the structure of power. That conditioning cannot be the last word is clear, for there have to be conditioners, and the awkward question remains, who conditions the conditioners? Who makes the ultimate, authoritative decisions? Who decides what stability is, and when it has been achieved? That government of some kind exists Huxley hints at. There are ten Controllers, we are told. But how exactly government works, how its power works, he does not go into. We can only assume that the competitive and aggressive elements of human nature have been removed not only from those in power but from those who might be candidates for power, while the perceptive and imaginative talents remain. Conditioning again? It is interesting to speculate on the possibilities of a test-tube revolution. One faulty product could distort the entire human race and the future of the world simply by tampering with the test tubes.

This is the most sombre aspect of the two books, the ease with which human nature can be dominated, whether by science or by brute power. Huxley and Orwell were both aware that within the society they observed, people were easily influenced. They were, in fact, being conditioned all the time, subjected all the time to pressures, mostly stemming from those with money and power, which were hard to resist. The test-tube baby and the Bokanovsky process are the logical extensions of brainwashing by advertisements and propaganda and official education. Big Brother is the logical extension of the uncritical acceptance of political power. What is in a sense revolutionary about both books is the concept that human nature can be changed, by whatever means, and changed not for the better, as traditional religions and idealisms have aimed for, but for the worse. Human nature has always responded to the suggestion that it can be improved, but in these books there is the suggestion that it might voluntarily co-operate in its debasement.

The Controller's arguments do not convince the Savage, who still wants freedom, even if it means freedom to kill himself. The suicide might be seen as the most powerful and independent action against the brave new world. That pain is a crucial element of uncivilized society the Reservation episodes make clear. Huxley is not trying to present savage society as a legitimate alternative to the sterile society, but he is saying that, in spite of all assumptions to the contrary, a painless society is not necessarily what should be aimed for. Amongst the savages pain, self-inflicted pain, has a ritualistic function. In the new world individuals are denied the freedom to create their own pain (and surely the programmers slipped up there, in discounting the psychological importance of pain) which is what Bernard is ineffectually seeking. He does not quite have the courage to take the plunge into the unknown experience, but when he is first told that he might be deported he is quite excited.

> Bernard left the room with a swagger, exulting, as he banged the door behind him, in the thought that he stood alone, embattled against the order of things; elated by the intoxicating consciousness of his individual significance and importance. Even the thought of persecution left him undismayed, was rather tonic than depressing. (Chapter 6)

Here he is with a chance to experience feelings that stability allowed only the smallest scope for. He is aware of himself as an individual, and when he tells his friend Helmholtz about it Huxley uses the word 'heroic', that anachronistic concept, to describe the nature of his account. For a brief moment Bernard is able to think of himself in an almost Shakespearian way, and we are aware of the fact that up till now in the novel this is just what he has been seeking. Until now he has been aware of himself as odd, as considered peculiar by others, but has not been able to give a name to his vague feelings of maladjustment. What he wants is an experience that will give this to him, an experience that will transform his oddity into genius, or heroism, or some other anachronistic quality.

Suffering without significance is not very much help. Bernard's inability to lose himself in communal activities, for instance, makes him feel miserable rather than an individualist. Isolation is not the same as individualism. What he feels is a terrible sense of being one apart.

He was as miserably isolated now as he had been when the service began—more isolated by reason of his unreplenished emptiness, his dead satiety. Separate and unatoned, while the others were being fused into the Greater Being; alone even in Morgana's embrace—much more alone, indeed, more hopelessly himself than he had ever been in his life before. He had emerged from the crimson twilight into the common electric glare with a self consciousness intensified to the pitch of agony. (Chapter 5)

He cannot *do* anything with his sense of separate identity; he is 'hopelessly himself'. Bernard's motivation throughout the book is an urge to transform his miserable separateness into heroic individualism. His visit to the Reservation and his decision to bring the Savage back to civilization are part of this, though also of a more infantile desire to confront the Director with the consequences of his youthful folly. But although he accomplishes the Savage's transfer he is not able to cope with the consequences, and at the moment of crisis he is totally demoralized. His conditioning, of course, has done nothing to equip him for things getting out of hand. Bernard contains within himself the seed of romanticism, of romantic self-awareness and suffering, but there is no room for growth. The seed is swiftly transplanted to a place of exile before it can establish itself—though in fact Bernard's real potential for challenging the system is not very great. He is exiled because he can't fit into the system rather than because he might actively attempt to destroy it.

So there is 'human nature' in Bernard, as there is in the Controller. They both want, or in the case of the Controller wanted in the past, more than they have, both feel an urge to get beyond the system. The Controller can be given responsibility because he can command his own nature. Bernard cannot. He cannot even be allowed a choice. Again, the possibility of choice is something that has been all but removed from life, and so its dangers are that much greater. People do not know how to choose. One of the basic tensions in society is that which arises from the need to maintain a balance between individual freedom and anti-social or destructive behaviour, and a great deal of what we consider characteristic of normal life stems from this, but there is no tension in the brave new world, and the individual who experiences it and refuses to take the prescribed antidote, *soma*, commits an offence. Primitive societies have been able to control this balance pretty well. The Savage comes from a society where there are ritual, if crude and primitive, methods of dealing with tension to a society where tension does not exist. He has absorbed a body of literature that has its roots in moral and social tensions. His situation is drastic while Bernard's is no more than mildly irritating. And it is intensified by the fact that even on the Reservation John was an outsider, a self-conscious individualist who had his head full of Shakespeare and was not wholly accepted. His self-awareness is baffled and blighted by what he sees in the brave new world, and none of the available opiates will work with him.

These opiates are sex and *soma*, assisted by the feelies, synthetic music, and sporting activities like clockwork golf. Savage society has its opiates too—Linda, John's mother, has been much reliant on sex and peyote. That every society has its methods of avoiding or beautifying reality is clear, and Huxley was attacking the opiates of his own contemporary society, instant entertainment, easy escapism, the things that keep people mindlessly happy. (Yet later he was to become intrigued with the way in which drugs can enhance the quality of vision and experience, and a non-addictive drug is an important feature of Pala society in *Island*.) But in *Brave New World* Huxley is concerned with the use of opiates as a weapon of manipulation. Having removed the need for responsibility and a moral sense (which Huxley witnessed those of his own generation deliberately trying to destroy or negate) sex is a way of channelling off any possible tensions and redundant energy that may be lurking in the human system. And having in its turn been deprived of all the tensions that normally surround it sex becomes something as readily available and achievable as perfume from a tap. Any anti-social sexual proclivities can be programmed out of the system.

Huxley visualizes sex as a means of consuming excess energy, Orwell sexual repression as a means of generating it. The mass-hysteria, the rallies, the chanting, the manipulated aggression which are a feature of Oceanic life are seen as the result of mass sexual frustration. Sex is discouraged, even within marriage. Winston recalls his wife's Party-induced frigidity. There is an Anti-Sex League to which all young people are encouraged to belong—Julia is a member. As repression has become an aim and a weapon of Ingsoc engineering, sexual union, as Winston reflects, has all the significance of a political act. In *Brave New World* sex means virtually nothing, in *Nineteen Eighty-Four* it means almost

The emotions it registered would be different from the ones he felt. (Part Three, 3)

What Orwell is actually describing here, I would guess, is the surviving inmate of a Nazi concentration camp. It would not be unfamiliar to readers who had seen photographs and newsreels. The passage goes on to describe Winston's physical condition still further, but the significant thing is the disunity of self, the lack of co-ordination and connection between the inner self and the outer body. '"We have broken you up,"' says O'Brien. The inability of the mind to work in unity with the body is a feature of the breaking up. As long as he stays alive the body exists, but the sense of self has been destroyed. At this stage, all that remains is his love for Julia, but that does not linger for long. The very fact that he thinks it is still important means that it will have to be destroyed. This love is Winston's last vestige of individualism, and when that has gone there is no hope of any value in memory remaining. Memory is meaningless. Everything that he and Julia have done becomes meaningless, any value that their actions and feelings might have had as ends in themselves is negated.

This is what the destruction of the individual means. The individual is just a cell in an organism, O'Brien explains. Expendable, renewable, its whole significance lying in its relation to the larger organism. When language, memory and feeling, the private resources of the individual have gone there is nothing left that can confirm an independent existence. In the end Winston gets his *ownlife* but there is nothing left of him to be aware of the value of being alone.

In *Brave New World* the elements of human life that have been lost are made quite clear. Savagery has been removed, but so have imagination and creativity. In *Nineteen Eighty-Four* it is much harder to trace the positive aspects of human nature that have been destroyed, although the fact of their destruction is so stark. There is no freedom, but what might be the positive results of freedom? Winston isn't clear. What elements of personality would the quality of life that Orwell hints at in the country episodes and in the junk-shop foster and encourage? Orwell is not condemning Ingsoc and totalitarianism because it does not allow great art, but because it does not allow simple private pleasures. Like Huxley, he is attacking the synthetic society but in what might be called more democratic terms than Huxley. He is not condemning the lack of

everything. Julia thinks of her revolt wholly in terms of sex. Every illicit relationship is a blow struck for self-expression. And the metaphor of aggression is apt. 'Their embrace had been a battle, the climax a victory. It was a blow struck against the Party. It was a political act,' Winston reflects after their first encounter. Sex is an act of aggression, against the Party perhaps, but involving the individuals themselves; it can also be a feature of moral corruption, of weakness. Desperately, Winston would like to think that the Inner Party is vulnerable, not super-human, not above temptation, for that would reveal a crucial weakness.

Anything that hinted at corruption always filled him with a wild hope. Who knew, perhaps the Party was rotten under the surface, its cult of strenuousness and self-denial simply a sham concealing inquity. If he could have inflicted the whole lot of them with leprosy or syphilis, how gladly he would have done so! Anything to rot, to weaken, to undermine! (Part Two, 2)

Ingsoc is beyond this stage of rather primitive rebellion. Behind their apparatus of power, moral corruption and rottenness can flourish and do no damage. As there are the means to make people believe whatever is required, it scarcely matters what the reality is.

It is the distortion of reality that is the most serious threat to human nature in *Nineteen Eighty-Four*. Individuality is damaged not merely by crude force, but by the destruction of history. There is nothing to sustain the individual, no rich environment of history and tradition, no growth, no developement. Huxley has conditioned the necessity for these things out of society, but in Orwell's interpretation there is still a disturbed consciousness of a lack. The conditioning process is still going on, in fact will go on for ever, for every time policy changes, the past has to be altered. Stability will never be achieved, and it is not desirable that it should be achieved. Human nature is not entirely destroyed, not fully controlled, which is why power has to be brutal and punishment drastic. Correctives will always be a part of a never-ending process, and there will always be rebels, for power itself is the end of power, and power must have victims. Without victims power is meaningless. The implications of this vision of power in its effect on human nature are significant, for Orwell's picture depends on a belief that there is, or has developed, a deep-rooted need for power for its own sake. Orwell himself believed this to be true; his observation and experience of war and totalitarianism confirmed it. But if this is true, then it is important that human nature is not destroyed. Its receptivity and its respect for power must always exist. For power to work, there must always be both O'Briens and Winston Smiths. This is the nightmare of 1984, a situation that will always be in the process of means, that will never arrive at ends, because it is the means that are important and the ends that are instrumental.

It was this situation, ideals used to justify power, that Orwell was attacking so fiercely, and attacked in various ways throughout his writing life. He does not show us the destruction of human nature in *Nineteen Eighty-Four*, but the terrible demoralization and degradation of human nature. In order to show us this, none of his central figures can be allowed considerable stature. If Winston Smith had been allowed to command more respect at the outset, his defeat could be seen as heroic, and that would have been contrary to the book's purpose. We must be shown a man, aware of his vulnerability and weakness, brought even lower than he was before.

Winston never thinks in heroic terms, as Bernard does, and as the Savage, fortified by Shakespeare, does. What he wants initially is 'normality', or something that he thinks must once have been normality. When he experiences disappointment on being told by Julia that their meeting has to be postponed, he thinks,

> It struck him that when one lived with a woman this particular disappointment must be normal, recurring event; and a deep tenderness, such as he had not felt for her before, suddenly took hold of him. He wished that they were a married couple of ten years' standing. He wished that he were walking through the streets with her just as they were doing now but openly and without fear, talking of trivialities and buying odds and ends for the household. He wished above all that they had some place where they could be alone together without feeling the obligation to make love every time they met. (Part Two, 4)

Mr Charrington's room is the attempt to achieve normality, but the decision to use it is as much a political act as their love-making, and their fear and their knowledge of punishment undermines the normality. And what is normality? Neither of them know. It is an instinctive feeling that produces Winston's responses to the peacefulness and beauty of the

summer countryside and the safety and comfort of Mr Charrington's room, an instinctive feeling that there is something deeply right and properly human about what they are doing.

For Winston's memories of the past, such as they are, fragmentary and unhappy, give him few pointers towards what human happiness might be. He remembers squalor, deprivation, selfishness, misery, nothing to suggest to him that the past was any better than the present except a dim feeling that his mother had a capacity for endurance, the same capacity that he detects in his observation of the proles. That Winston's memories are of 1948 or soon after is quite clear. In 1984 he is thirty-nine years old, and it is his childhood he is trying to reconstruct. The fact that Orwell provides us with so direct a link with the time in which he was writing is revealing, a confirmation of nearness of 1948 to 1984.

Society is not controlled entirely by fear. There is a manipulated system of rewards and opiates. There is Victory Gin. There are mass rallies and public hangings and the Two Minutes Hate which serve the double purpose of allowing the individual to forget himself and strengthening the pillars of power. There are cinemas and community organizations which have a similar function. There is synthetic literature and, for the proles, pornography. These are the instruments of defeating self-awareness and conquering individualism. At the end of the book we witness Winston's loss of all control over his own personality. His mind has to accept that he is himself, yet self has been obliterated, self cannot be allowed to exist. He exists, yet does not exist. It is a contradiction he has to accept, just as he has to accept that two and two make five. And not only does he have to accept, he has to *believe* that there is no irrationality involved. At the end of the penultimate stage of his 'rehabilitation' this is how he sees himself.

> A bowed, grey-coloured skeleton-like thing was coming towards him. Its actual appearance was frightening, and not merely the fact that he knew it to be himself. He moved closer to the glass. The creature's face seemed to be protruded, because of its bent carriage. A forlorn, jailbird's face with a nobby forehead running back into a bald scalp, a crooked nose, and battered-looking cheekbones above which the eyes were fierce and watchful. The cheeks were seamed, the mouth had a drawn-in look. Certainly it was his own face, but it seemed to him that it had changed more than he had changed inside.

suitable environment for the great, but the lack of a suitable environment for the ordinary. Which is another reason why Winston cannot be allowed to be too special. Unlike Bernard, Winston must be 'the common man'—a figure that cannot possibly exist in Huxley's new society. Winston's destruction is the destruction of the common man, while the exile of Bernard is the exile of the potentially exceptional. We could compare the use of Shakespeare in *Brave New World* with the use of nursery rhymes in *Nineteen Eighty-Four*, the great product of an individual imagination compared with the anonymous products of the folk. It is a useful metaphor for the tendencies of the two writers.

All Winston's attempts to suggest to himself an alternative to the current way of life are extremely tentative, and after his arrest and torture assume the quality of dream. He calls the country of his dreams the Golden Country, and it is a place of sunlight, stillness and peace, but with every suggestion of feasibility wiped out. It is like the 'old world' George Bowling sets out to rediscover. Perhaps these Golden Countries never did exist and never can exist. For Winston, the ability, even the desire, to dream will disappear, and Winston will have submitted entirely to Big Brother's version of reality. Bernard will in exile, it is suggested, find some scope for nourishing his oddness, in a situation where it can do no damage to himself or to the fabric of society. There is nothing like that for Winston. It is the difference between human nature becoming redundant, and human nature destroyed.

We need to know what the result of either eventuality might be. That is the need that perpetuates the importance of both these books in spite of the fact that neither of them offer us what is generally sought for in fiction. Any curiosity about personality and independence is bound to extend to the possibility of their extinction. Other novels, perhaps, tell us about the vulnerability of human nature. These novels tell us how life can go on without it, and how such an eventuality can be seen as progress. Orwell's faith in the resilience of human nature, which he genuinely felt most of the time and is expressed elsewhere, led to his understanding of how easy it is for men and women to accept the unacceptable. Resilience, tolerance, cheerfulness in adversity, are good qualities with which to fight and win a war, but Orwell saw that the habit of responding to the excessive demands of an emergency could lead to an acceptance of authority, whatever form that authority took. Would the Britons who remained cheerful during the extremities of war have maintained their cheerfulness under the extremities of Hitler? If they had, would we see it as encouraging or disastrous? Hope lies with the proles because they can still sing as they go about their menial tasks—but does that not mean also that they are probably just happy enough *not* to rebel?

4. Politics

When *Nineteen Eighty-Four* was published many readers read the book as a statement of Orwell's rejection of socialism. That it was never intended to be this most critics now agree, but the fact that it could be read in that way, and was even embraced by the political right wing as a weapon for their cause, poses a problem. Shortly after the book was published Isaac Deutscher wrote an article in which he attacked Orwell for writing a book that was politically dangerous. *Nineteen Eighty-Four*, he considered, could be used as a weapon by those who did not understand the author's intentions, or who deliberately distorted them. It offered political ideas that could readily be turned into slogans, a political vocabulary that had made 'frantic incursions' into the English language. For these reasons Deutscher considered *Nineteen Eighty-Four* to be a dangerous book.

That it made an immediate and striking impression on the public imagination there is no doubt, and it did so both through the relevance and reality of what it contained and through its extremity of tone. 'Big Brother' and 'doublethink' *did* enter the English language. The flavour and tendency of the book have become common knowledge. The passage of time, I think, has made some considerable difference to the viability of Deutscher's view, which was expressed when the Cold War was still a reality and Hitler fresh in the memory. We read *Nineteen Eighty-Four* now not so much for its specifically political message as for what it has to say about human vulnerability in the face of political power and, above all, the manipulation of history. Yet having said that, it is important to point out that that contains, fundamentally, Orwell's political message, and that, in spite of first reactions to the book, to see it at all in terms of right wing and left is a distortion.

Orwell maintained that every worthwhile piece of writing he produced had a political intention, but we should not interpret that as meaning that he had a party-political case to make. He was highly suspicious of political parties, and was himself the member of one, the Independent Labour Party, for only a very brief period. We could perhaps rephrase what Orwell himself claimed, and say that he never failed to write with a *moral* purpose, but that he saw morality, realistically and rightly I would argue, in political terms. He was a political writer because he recognized the way in which political power influenced the lives and aspirations of ordinary people.

The object of political power in Oceania is to eliminate memory and self-consciousness in order to perpetuate political power. 'Orthodoxy was unconsciousness' is the way in which Orwell sums it up. Winston comes face to face with the paradox implied in that.

> The Party said that Oceania had never been in alliance with Eurasia. He, Winston Smith, knew that Oceania had been in alliance with Eurasia as short a time as four years ago. But where did that knowledge exist? Only in his own consciousness, which in any case must soon be annihilated. And if all the others accepted the lie which the Party imposed—if all records told the same tale—then the lie passed into history and became truth. 'Who controls the past,' ran the Party slogan, 'controls the future: who controls the present controls the past.' And yet the past, though of its nature alterable, never had been altered. Whatever was true now had been true from everlasting to everlasting. It was quite simple. All that was needed was an unending series of victories over your own memory. (Part One, 3)

Orwell demonstrates how the victories over memory are achieved. Winston is aware of the fact that the Party can alter the unalterable at the same time as making everyone believe that the unalterable has never been altered. His awareness is fatal, a flaw in the system, yet not a serious flaw for the system can rectify it perfectly easily, as the book shows. The Party actually incorporates the paradox into its philosophy by inventing the concept 'double think'.

> To know and not to know, to be conscious of complete truthfulness while telling carefully constructed lies, to hold simultaneously two opinions which cancelled out, knowing them to be contradictory and believing in both of them; to use logic against logic, to repudiate morality while laying claim to it, to believe that democracy was impossible and that the Party was the guardian of democracy; to

forget whatever it was necessary to forget, then to draw it back into memory again at the moment when it was needed, and then promptly to forget it again: and above all to apply the same process to the process itself. That was the ultimate subtlety: consciously to induce unconsciousness, and then, once again, to become unconscious of the act of hypnosis you had just performed. Even to understand the word 'doublethink' involved the use of doublethink. (Part One, 3)

The process Orwell is exposing here is that which allowed Stalin, for instance, to announce the Nazi/Soviet Pact in 1938 as if he and Hitler had always been the best of friends. Doublethink gives the Party absolute control. It is a much more subtle and complex process than simply using threats to impose a creed. Smoothly operated it requires an instant change of gear the moment, or even a hairsbreadth in anticipation of, a change of line is announced. Brutality is a significant political weapon, but there comes a point when it is no longer necessary. When doublethink has been fully achieved, when people can employ and eliminate the process simultaneously, the revolution is complete and force is merely an expression of power, not a means to an end: except that perhaps doublethink *can't* operate effectively without an intimate knowledge of the reality of force.

Newspeak is an important element in this. Its object is to boil language down to its ultimate reduction. Language is also a weapon, but again once doublethink has been perfected, the necessity for language other than the language of doublethink becomes minimal. Thinking and feeling, even communicating, become wholly irrelevant concepts. The basic relationship between the State and its citizens is the relationship between power and its victims, the boot stamping everlastingly on a face, as O'Brien puts it later in the book. That is the only significant relationship, and it can scarcely be called human. Power has to be given a human face, Big Brother on the poster, but that is only because it needs to be identified, and the victim must confirm the relationship by loving its source. The victim must be willing. Doublethink is a means of making the victim willing.

Winston's job is the rewriting of history. He has to alter the documentation of the past so that it will conform to the current interpretation of the present. If Oceania changes sides it must be established that it has always been on the side it changes to. The process is somewhat crude. Altering documentation seems an elaborate way of rewriting history in a society where documents are not important anyway. Who will read the old newspapers that Winston meticulously alters? But of course it is no more crude than the kind of juggling with facts that politics frequently entails. Winston as a rewriter must not be aware of himself as altering facts, but of correcting errors. But he is not submissive enough to doublethink to be unaware of exactly what he is doing.

If there are any conspicuous flaws in the instant alteration of history—for instance, the wrong slogans on the posters when policy is changed in mid-speech at a vast rally—these can be blamed on the enemy's underground spies and agents. And in order to maintain the useful belief in enemy agents, periodically people have to be arrested and purged for that particular crime. Fear is a key weapon. People must be made to believe that they can inadvertently commit crimes, and they must also believe that even their own thoughts belong to the State. People disappear and are never heard of again. There are occasional public trials of arch enemies. Above all, no one can be allowed to feel secure.

At its crudest, power is the manipulation of primitive emotion. Every element of thought and feeling can be eliminated except for the crudest form of hatred and mass hysteria. The communal hysteria of the Two Minutes Hate, the orgiastic Hate Week, are ways in which Big Brother can be loved. Huxley all but kills emotion, but Orwell describes a situation in which near-animal emotion is the only significant human expression. That he drew to a great extent on the spectacle of the massive Fascist rallies and the abject, masochistic confessions of the Moscow Trials is quite clear. Before Hitler the potential of the mass rally had never been fully explored. No one who has heard a recording of a Hitler rally, or seen a film, can have escaped the *frisson* that comes from the terrifying spectacle and sound of thousands of voices joined in unthinking emotion, thousands reacting like automatons to the bidding of a single man. It was mass ritual pushed to its furthest extremes. Orwell saw what it could do, and in recognizing its power over vast numbers of people could contemplate a situation in which it was a major expression and prop of power. Power both feeds mass hysteria, and is fed by it.

In order to maintain the purity of these crude, animal responses, the Party destroys everything that could give individuals any illusion of independence, or pride, or spiritual sustenance. There must be no way of satisfying private needs—there must be no private needs. Daily existence is stripped of all possible colour or variation or pleasure. The necessities of life are stripped to the minimal requirements, and the basic acts of eating, drinking and love-making are made to seem as unpleasant as possible. The canteen where Winston eats is disgusting, with its sour smell, spilt food, almost inedible stew, oily-tasting gin, a grim, noisy, overcrowded environment (based, it has been said, on the BBC canteen in wartime!) which removes any pleasure there might possibly be in satisfying the appetite. This stripping process induces a submissive population, and a population more receptive to synthetic, State-controlled entertainment. Inner resources are whittled away, for they cannot flourish in the desert which the State has created, and thus dependence on the State is increased.

But why, is the question we and Winston inevitably ask? What is it all for? O'Brien asks this same question of Winston in the final pages of the book, but his answer is naïve, though the one that most of us would produce. Winston says that the Party needs to maintain power for the good of the majority, that all these unpleasantnesses are a means to an end, that the end is the happiness of mankind, which is more important than freedom, that only the Party is able to understand and achieve what is good. This, Winston thought, and millions of others have thought, was the justification of power. It was the justification that Orwell had witnessed being used by Hitler, by Stalin, by Franco, and, though so different in degree, by Roosevelt and by Churchill. The end justifies the means, the equation that has so fascinated and disturbed Orwell's contemporary Arthur Koestler, who had had a more intimate experience of its effects. But O'Brien contradicts all that, and by contradicting it throws doubt on all possible uses of that rationalization of power.

A number of readers have criticized Orwell for his inclusion of a large chunk of the theoretical exposure of Ingsoc, the invented Goldstein's *Theory and Practice of Oligarchical Collectivism*. It is necessary, though, for the theories and the motives and the origins of Ingsoc to be described, just as the theory of stability, as well as the practice, must be demonstrated in *Brave New World*. By the time we reach this stage in the book we have been given a taste of the methods and we have seen Winston's and Julia's tentative rebellion. The introduction of a further dimension to what we know of the political structure is important. In effect, the Goldstein passages explain how and why it is that in 1948 Ingsoc seemed more probable than Huxley's brave new world.

> The world of today is a bare, hungry, dilapidated place compared with the world that existed before 1914, and still more so if compared with the imaginary future to which people of that period looked forward. In the early twentieth century, the vision of a future society unbelievably rich, leisured, orderly, and efficient—a glittering, antiseptic world of glass and steel and snowwhite concrete—was part of the consciousness of nearly every literate person. Science and technology were developing at a prodigious speed, and it seemed natural to assume that they would go on developing. This failed to happen, partly because of the impoverishment caused by a long series of wars and revolutions, partly because scientific and technical progress depended on the empirical habit of thought, which could not survive in a strictly regimented society. As a whole the world is more primitive today than it was fifty years ago. (Part Two, 9)

This explains the defeat of science, a case Orwell has to put, and the theory goes on to explain that science is only necessary to develop armaments which are needed to pursue warfare, the primary aim of which is 'to use up the products of the machine without raising the general standard of living'. War is a method not of defeating another nation, for the war must not be allowed to end, but of defeating the people, the mass of society, not necessarily by killing them, but by making life as minimal as possible. 'The essential act of war is destruction, not necessarily of human lives, but of the products of human labour. War is a way of shattering to pieces, or pouring into the stratosphere, or sinking in the depths of the sea, materials which might otherwise be used to make the masses too comfortable, and hence, in the long run, too intelligent.' But why make the materials, why not simply put an end altogether to an industrialized society? Manufacture has to go on because labour is a means of slavery, an instrument of power, and *productive* labour is a psychological necessity. Simply digging holes in the ground or building useless monuments would provide 'only the economic and not the emotional basis for a hierarchical society'. In order for Party members to remain fanatically loyal, which is what power requires, they must believe in the reality and the necessity of war and the necessity for production and hard work. There must be conspicuous consumption so that there can be conspicuous effort.

The Theory and Practice of Oligarchical Collectivism is carefully and convincingly worked out, and that plus Orwell's appendix on Newspeak show his impressive grasp of the psychology of politics. The structure of power, the manipulation of people and history, the function and misuse of language, had been preoccupations of Orwell's for all of his writing life. In *Nineteen Eighty-Four* they are fiercely crystallized into an alarming emotional and intellectual whole. But the ultimate explanation is not provided until very near the end of the book. In his reading of Goldstein, Winston reaches the passage where the motive power is about to be explained, when his and Julia's illusory peace is shattered by the Thought Police. Reality takes over from the written word.

It is a brilliantly contrived moment in the novel. Winston has been reading aloud to Julia. First Julia, then he himself, falls asleep. Winston awakes to a new awareness of beauty, a fresh understanding of hope. The sky is cloudless, the birds are singing and the proles, Winston, feels, are immortal—'they would stay alive against all the odds, like birds, passing on from body to body the vitality which the Party did not share and could not kill'. And as long as he can keep that thought alive in his mind he can share some of the hope for the future. But the thought does not survive for long. Immediately the arrest takes place, the process of killing the mind begins. The hope, if it exists, is an objective hope. Neither the proles nor, in the end, Winston, are aware of it, and if the hope cannot actually function in the minds and imaginations of individuals it doesn't really exist. Winston has broken off in midsentence in his reading of Goldstein, just when he was going to learn about power. And then there is 'a stampede of boots up the stairs. The room was full of solid men in black uniforms, with iron-shod boots on their feet and truncheons in their hands.' This is their first direct experience of brute force. This, as O'Brien will later explain, is power and the object of power, the boot stamping on a human face. The black uniforms and iron boots *are* what power is about.

When Winston offers the answer, '"You are ruling over us for our own good"', O'Brien has one more lesson to teach him, the most crucial lesson of all.

We are not interested in the good of others; we are interested solely in power. Not wealth or luxury or long life or happiness: only power, pure power. . . . Power is not a means to an end. One does not establish a dictatorship in order to safeguard a revolution; one makes the revolution in order to establish the dictatorship. The object of persecution is persecution. The object of torture is torture. The object of power is power. (Part Three, 3)

If there is a flaw in Orwell's thesis it is that there is a gap in the rationality of this final lesson. Of course, his argument is that humanity can be forced to accept the irrational along with anything else. (In *Darkness at Noon* Koestler had shown how rationality could be prevented without losing its logic). If thought processes can be ignored, destroyed, done away with, overridden, distorted, what possible weapon is left for the individual? The only answer in *Nineteen Eighty-Four* is that life, in some sort of recognizable way, goes on; hope lies with the proles. They love and marry and breed and grow prematurely old. It comes back to human nature. Orwell does seem to be suggesting that human nature, in some primitive form, will continue to survive, and that eventually out of that might grow imaginative thought strong enough to challenge Big Brother.

The proles exist as they do not because the Party can't control them but because it can't be bothered. The Party destroys any oddities and anyone with dangerous potential, but does not consider the survival of human nature on the level of the proles as worth worrying about. From this stems Winston's belief that hope lies with the proles. But in *Brave New World* there is no hope of anything different, because society is carefully modulated to find a suitable niche for all levels of consciousness. There is a place and a function for everyone and everyone, virtually, is happy with that place and function. Even the Savage Reservation is so thoroughly extraterritorial, and confined, that it is of no more danger than a zoo in a large city. The Savage's eccentric behaviour in civilization causes a bit of a ripple, but nothing that is seriously disturbing, and there is no suggestion that the climactic orgy has any ill effects on anyone other than the Savage himself. Far from it, for it simply follows a ritual that has been standardized by civilization, although in the earlier stages there seems to be a dangerous curiosity about self-inflicted pain, an oddity indeed in a society where pain has been eliminated and indicative perhaps of a lingering primitive need.

In both novels the destruction of traditional units of cohesion is a basic requirement. Family relationships, sexual relationships, any kind of relationship that demands loyalty and trust, have to be destroyed so that the loyalty and trust can be directed towards the State—or whatever word is used to describe the whole of which the individual is a part. The State in a political sense may appear not to exist in *Brave New World*, but of course it does, there *is* a political structure, a power structure, although it is not precisely defined. Without small units of self-support the individual is vulnerable, the State powerful. (Decentralization as a means of dispersing power was an important belief of Huxley's.) In *Brave New World* individuals are not aware of their vulnerability. They adhere naturally to the values of the State, for their conditioning removes the need to look for any alternative. What is interesting in *Brave New World* is that there is no need for the State to demonstrate its power overtly, or to demand the extrovert demonstration of loyalty from its citizens. It has no competition, and its structure does not depend on mass hysterical commitment as does the power structure in *Nineteen Eighty-Four*.

One of Bernard's problems is that although he is discontented and critical he has no idea what, if anything, can be done about it. Winston begins a process of reconstruction that suggests to him an alternative, and his reading of Goldstein helps, but by then it is too late. Just as he thinks he is going to learn what might be done he discovers the hard way that nothing can be done. Bernard does not seriously consider the Savage Reservation as an alternative to civilization as he knows it. He finds it all rather crude and disgusting, as indeed it is, and Huxley emphasizes his dependence on the technology of civilization as an ironic reinforcement of his response. Bernard would be helpless as a savage, while Winston would survive amongst the proles. 'Civilization' gives him nothing that he wants.

Bernard's fears are not of torture and death but of humiliation or, at the worst, comfortable exile. Yet the fears are real. He is terrified of being overheard as he talks to Helmholtz in the privacy of the latter's room. He cannot bear the thought that he might be unorthodox. His attitude to his own oddness is ambivalent. He hates it, but he wants to do something with it. Later, when he has been reinforced by his success with the Savage, he boasts of his unorthodoxy. Both attitudes are equally foolish, yet symptomatic of his uneasy awareness of maladjustment. When he and Helmholtz talk both are conscious of performing an anti-social act, but neither are quite aware of what this might mean in terms of social structure or their own places in it. Helmholtz is aware of the emptiness of what he is doing—'Can you write something about nothing?' he wonders—but he does not question the necessity of his job in such a way as to enable him to change the direction of his work.

The social structure of society is based entirely on production and consumption. It is a logical extension of the capitalist consumer society that Huxley experienced in the 1920s. The lower castes produce, the higher castes maintain the engineering that keeps the lower castes happily producing, and they all consume, although of course the higher more than the lower. There is no economic problem, because no one wants more than they have. There is room for a certain amount of ambition amongst the Alphas, as the motivation is useful, but not amongst the lower castes. The lower your caste the more permanently are you fixed.

The whole of life is geared to economic consumption. Anything that was free, that might be enjoyed for nothing, has been obliterated. Wild flowers, for instance, as the Director explains.

> Primroses and landscapes, he pointed out, have one grave defect: they are gratuitous. A love of nature keeps no factories busy. It was decided to abolish the love of nature, at any rate among the lower classes; to abolish the love of nature, but *not* the tendency to consume transport. For of course it was essential that they should keep on going to the country, even though they hated it. The problem was to find an economically sounder reason for consuming transport than a mere affection for primroses and landscapes. (Chapter 2)

The answer is sport, which has been developed to require more and more expensive equipment so that it can take its place in the cycle of conspicuous consumption. In *Brave New World* it is consumption that makes the world go round. There is constant encouragement to replace the old with the new, to be always doing things and going places. The discouragement of isolated activity is not just psychological, not only a weapon to bolster the State, but a part of the consumer ideology. Those who read books or talk to each other in the privacy of their own rooms or go for walks in the Lake District are not consuming. Leisure is consumption. Work is the stabilization of the environment for consumption, at least for the Alphas. For the lower caste it is constant, repetitive production of things to be consumed. And although this part of the lesson the Alphas are taught as they lie in their cots, and although

Bernard has anti-social instincts, he is not able to focus them on the right cause. In a sense he loves the system in the same way that Winston, ultimately, loves Big Brother.

Again it is a question of alternatives. There are none. Party politics would be a futile disruption of a smoothly running system, entirely unnecessary and unproductive—although the Party political process would consume. The class structure is stabilized, the power structure is stabilized and the economic structure is stabilized. Stability is the aim and object of the whole system, and the dissatisfied customer is a rarity. The quality of life is part of the engineering required to maintain stability, and the purpose of maintaining stability is simply to perpetuate stability. There is nothing creative in the structure, no question of there being aims or goals to be moved towards; self-perpetuation is all. The situation is the same in *Nineteen Eighty-Four*, of course, a signal feature of totalitarianism although that word was not current when Huxley was writing. Totalitarianism is a process of self-perpetuation, and what it performs in terms of legislation or enactment is for that purpose. Orwell's recognition of this is symbolized in his picture of power for its own sake. It is power for the sake of continuing to be powerful. In *Brave New World* there is stability for the sake of continuing to be stable.

The conditioning involved in *Brave New World* is moral not factual. The Director explains how the attempt to convey facts through hypnopaedia failed, for they could not be remembered in any meaningful way. But the conveyance of attitudes was a complete success: '"Wordless conditioning is crude and wholesale; cannot bring home the finer distinctions, cannot inculcate the more complex courses of behaviour. For that there must be words, but words without reason."' (Chapter 2) Even Alphas are not taught how or why, simply to accept what they are and be what they accept. Facts are not necessary, indeed they are an interference. History is wiped out. Education, post-conditioning education, is simply a process of propelling children along the groove for which they have already been conditioned. (Huxley does not explain precisely how job allocation works, but we can presume that future occupation is established at a very early stage. Even amongst the Alphas except for those at the very top, jobs require very little more than a mechanical functioning. As we have seen, technology *could* make even some Alphas redundant.)

History has been wiped out because it is irrelevant, not because, as in

Nineteen Eighty-Four, it is dangerous. Doublethink makes history meaningless, because alterable; stability makes history meaningless because anything that is essentially about processes of change and development can have nothing to offer a stable society that is never going to change and need have no curiosity about how it got where it did. How to stay there matters, but not how it got there. One or two selected lessons are preserved from the not too distant post-revolutionary past, the Cyprus experiment for instance. But, as the Controller says, no previous civilization can have any interest at all to a stable present. At best, history can be a horror story, rather the same experience as a visit to the Savage Reservation. But as long as there is a Savage Reservation no one needs history. If people need to be reminded of what they are not, it is easily done.

The manipulation of the past is a crux, as much in *Brave New World* as in *Nineteen Eighty-Four*. It is almost impossible to contemplate the imagination functioning without relating continuously to the past, or to a future that is likely to be different in some way from the past. That a degree of political control might be achieved that would alter or obliterate the past and control the future absolutely is about as horrifying a prophetic vision as could be arrived at. That any situation might be possible in which technology dominates man rather than man technology is alarming—but in that respect we are considerably nearer brave new world than Huxley was, although he saw so clearly the implications of rapid developments in science and technology. In *Island* Huxley describes a society in which there is a minimum of technology, and all that there is is of direct use to human welfare, electricity for instance, and plant breeding. Electricity is a basic source of energy, plants of food. For human requirements to be reduced to such a simple level, the maintaining of diet, health, heat and light, is unthinkable in brave new world terms, for Pala is an anti-consumer, anti-caste society. But even Pala can't solve all the anomalies. There is still money. There is still buying and selling. And the admirable methods of dealing with friction and tension, a kind of harnessing of the best in primitive ritualism plus the use of a non-addictive drug, while coping with destructive anti-social behaviour might also be liable to deaden creative instincts in a way similar to Huxley's earlier utopia. It is clear that Huxley is aware of this, for he emphasizes the existence of disturbing feelings and situations that require the strenuous use of individual inner resources. Death and disease, for instance, are both very much present in his narrative. To make use of both social and individual resources requires self-consciousness, will-power, and a sense of social morality which are virtually absent from new world society.

One of the things that worries the Savage is the lack of self-denial, the lack of a demand for courage and endurance, the lack of tests, which for him are essential methods of coping with life. We have seen that Bernard vaguely felt that he would like to enlarge his experience in this direction—'Often in the past he had wondered what it would be like to be subjected (*soma*-less and with nothing but his own resources to rely on) to some great trial, some pain, some persecution; he had even longed for affliction'—perhaps because he has a suspicion that they might actually be of value in themselves. The kind of endurance and self-denial the Savage has in mind has been ritualized by uncivilized society. We have already been shown the demonstrations in the Reservation episodes. Remove the need, and of course the rituals themselves are valueless. But the need in the new world has not been entirely removed. There *are* still rituals, communal rituals not all that different from those on the Reservation, and there is still a need for a kind of religious sense, for the apprehension of something larger than the individual. The Solidarity orgies are the vehicles of this, and the focus is the State, but the State as something vast and mysterious and magnetic. As religion is conventionally an alternative to the State, the State, in *Nineteen Eighty-Four* also, absorbs religious feeling and uses it in its own support. The psychological necessity of religious feeling is recognized, its use as a means of release, reassurance, and out-of-the-ordinary experience, but it is only allowed to function within given terms.

Of course Huxley intends us to see the similarity between the apparently barbarous rituals on the Reservation and the orgies of the civilized—the climax of the book is a combination of the two. The orgy uses certain primitive instincts in the same way as Big Brother. But self-denial and courage are not seen as instincts but as a kind of Pavlovian reaction to deprivation. Industrial civilization, the Controller maintains, 'is only possible when there's no self-denial. Self-indulgence up to the very limits imposed by hygiene and economics. Otherwise the wheels may stop turning.' (Chapter 17) One has only to glance at some of the more striking features of the Industrial Revolution and the Victorian period of industrial expansion to know that this is not in fact true. But in terms of stability it is true—once stability has been achieved, *then* you need permanent self-indulgence, not self-denial, and if self-indulgence and religious worship can be combined, then the result is very satisfactory for the maintenance of the status quo.

Sex, private or communal, is the only outlet for what we would think of as human instinct, and is at the core of religious expression. There is no outlet for aggression, except perhaps through sport, but Huxley provides us with no details here. Any suggestion that sex is itself aggressive or competitive has been removed, for everyone is available to everyone else. This absence might seem rather curious, as it might be thought that aggression is as natural an impulse as sex, and it raises the question of whether it would in fact be possible to condition all tendencies towards competitiveness out of the human system. In the Controller's explanation the only important natural instinct is the sexual one, and the implication is that it supplants the need for anything else. If the indulgent instincts are allowed free play, the more painful ones will lapse anyway, is the suggestion that lies behind the argument.

> . . . civilization has absolutely no need of nobility or heroism. These things are symptoms of political inefficiency. In a properly organized society like ours, nobody has any opportunities for being noble or heroic. Conditions have got to be thoroughly unstable before the occasion can arise. Where there are wars, where there are divided allegiances, where there are temptations to be resisted, objects of love to be fought for or defended—there, obviously, nobility and heroism have some sense. But there aren't any wars nowadays. The greatest care is taken to prevent you from loving anyone too much. There's no such thing as a divided allegiance; you're so conditioned that you can't help doing what you ought to do. And what you ought to do is on the whole so pleasant, so many of the natural impulses are allowed free play, that there really aren't any temptations to resist. (Chapter 17)

In *Nineteen Eighty-Four* aggression as a natural impulse is both recognized and exploited, but there is no more point in heroism that there is in Huxley's book. That is the lesson Winston learns. Heroism is an individualist gesture which must be destroyed. Bernard may have some idea that he wants to be a hero, but he can't do it—there is no environment for heroism and absolutely no object. What could a potential hero in the brave new world actually do? Not much, as Bernard discovers when he gets over the brief honeymoon of fame that the Savage brings him. As for the Savage himself, it is his realization of this desert of human potential that leads him to reject civilization. Ironically it is his action on this discovery that finally puts a stop to any heroic daydreaming Bernard might have indulged in.

Huxley scarcely mentions the word politics. What meaning can the word have in a situation where all that is required has been achieved and the discussion about means is an anachronism? Yet *Brave New World* is about social structure and the organization of human life and it contains, inevitably, a political message. The message is, essentially, as anti-totalitarian and as morally concerned with the future of humanity as Orwell's. Both books were written out of the same impulse to protect the individual and to protect history. Their differences belong mostly to the specific periods in which they were written, their similarities to this shared impulse, a valid one whenever the time, present or future. It is possible now that their notoriety will be allowed to fade; that can't be regretted so long as their real achievement continues to be acknowledged, and the fact that both books have become, appropriately, an irreplaceable part of this century's culture.

Further Reading

One can't do better than to read more of both Huxley and Orwell, for instance:

Huxley: *Ends and Means* 1937
        Ape and Essence 1953
        Brave New World Revisited 1958
        Island 1962
        all published by Chatto and Windus, who also published *Brave New World*.

Orwell: *Homage to Catalonia* 1939
        Animal Farm 1945
        Collected Essays, Journalism and Letters 1968
        all published by Secker and Warburg, and Penguin, who also published *Nineteen Eighty-Four*.

George Woodcock has written good and helpful books on both writers: on Orwell, *The Crystal Spirit*, 1967, and on Huxley, *Dawn and the Darkest Hour*, Faber 1972. Peter Bowering's *Aldous Huxley*, Athlone Press 1968, discusses the novels in relation to Huxley's ideas and interests. There has now been so much written on Orwell it is hard to select. Two useful collections of critical essays are Stephen Hynes, editor, *Twentieth Century Interpretations of 1984*, Spectrum 1971, and Raymond Williams, editor, *George Orwell: a Collection of Critical Essays*, Prentice-Hall 1974.

Index